THE YEAR OF OBEDIENCE

Encouraging You to Walk Into What God Is Calling You to Do

ERIN LONON

PUBLISHERS

ISBN: 978-1-953759-10-8

This book is dedicated to my sisters, Ty and Cole, for encouraging me to journal this season of my life.

Acknowledgements

First and foremost, I give honor to God, who is everything and more to me. Four years ago, I was at the lowest season of my life, and I remember saying, "God, if you get me out of this, it's just You and me." Since that time, my life has changed in every single way. I will continue to remain obedient to Your Word and will always give you my best. God orchestrates every detail of my life, and throughout this year, I was reminded that He literally sees all things.

To my family, I would first like to thank my mom; you are my biggest cheerleader and supporter. Making it through this year of my life and writing this book would not have been possible without you. You never allowed me to quit, and you always found the time to edit and make revisions for me. If I become half the woman, wife, and mother you are, then I would have accomplished much in my life.

Secondly, to my dad and brothers, you three have always encouraged me to step out of my comfort zone and never settle to be mediocre. Hearing you all say, "That was good," will always be something I strive for.

To Amari and Leighton, you both literally are my "why." The days I wanted to quit but did not happened because you were my reminders that there are always people who are watching you. I want my life to be an example for you to always trust God and step out in faith.

To Aunt Shirley and Uncle Jack, thank you for believing in this vision and being my extra set of eyes when I needed them.

To my dream team: Kiana - you were the first person I told about this vision, and from that day on, you have always encouraged me. At my lowest moments, you spoke life into me, spoke tough love to me when I needed to hear it, and always showed up. I will forever cherish you and our friendship. Ty, Cole, Kelly, and Mrs. Lil, each of you are fearfully and wonderfully made. Thank you for not only trusting in this vision but for coming along with me on this journey. I will be forever grateful to each of you and know that God has amazing plans for each of your lives. Ladies, let us continue to move God's kingdom forward.

To my Grace City youth, you are all my heart. You keep me young, current, on my toes, but, most importantly, you keep me accountable. I think twice about my daily decisions because I always have you in the back of my mind. Thank you for teaching me more than I could have ever taught you. You make me better.

Lastly, but certainly not least, to every person who will read this book, thank you for taking a chance on me. My prayer for you is that you will step into what God is calling you to do, and you will see His work manifested through you when you say "yes" to Him. God really does all things well!

Table of Contents

Introduction

On the twenty first of September 2019, I attended a Bible study meeting. During our time together, we did an activity on hearing from the Holy Spirit. Our Bible study leader began by giving each woman a category and then assigning us a partner. Some of the categories included colors, personality, characteristics, and animals. Based on the category, we had to tell our partner what we felt we were hearing from the Holy Spirit pertaining to them. I did not really understand the activity at first, but once we started, the outcome was interesting. The category of animals came up, and the woman who I was partnered with said, "I do not know why but the animal that I feel like I am hearing for you is *dog*."

What? Really? A dog? I thought to myself. *What is that supposed to mean? Was she trying to call me a name?* Our Bible study leader said to my partner: "Well, let's break down the characteristics of a dog."

Yes, let's definitely do that! I thought.

When she began to break this thing down, I was literally in shock. She said, "Dogs are *obedient*, and they submit and are loyal to their master. They are able to attack but can also practice restraint." When I heard these words, I was literally in awe. I was thinking, *how did she know?* These exact characteristics were what I was walking through thus far in 2019. Hearing it in the Bible study was just another confirmation that God saw me.

So, my questions to you are, "What do you think about when you hear the term obedient? Would you consider yourself an obedient person?" Maybe you have never really thought about it, and until 2019 I had not either. However, I always knew one person who I admired for their obedience, and that was Abraham. Abraham was a man who is introduced to us in the first chapter of the Bible, Genesis. I always admired him because he lived a life that was fueled by obedience. I always wanted to have faith like Abraham. However, little did I know that the year 2019 was going to allow me the chance to follow in Abraham's footsteps.

As you open this book, I am not sure what year this is for you or what your year looks like. Maybe it is 2021, and you are just excited that 2020 has ended, and you are looking forward to a fresh start. Maybe it is 2025, and you have gone through a year of stretching and pruning, and you are hoping to see a harvest. Whatever year it is for you, I can tell you: this can also be your **YEAR OF OBEDIENCE**.

Let us get this journey started!

Chapter 1
Answer the Call

*"****E****rin, 2019 will be your year of obedience. This year I need you to be obedient to what I have called you to do."* It was the end of 2018, and I was having quiet time with the Lord when I heard Him say those exact words. Not really understanding what that meant, I said, *"Okay, Lord, I will be obedient to whatever You have called me to do."* That was it. No further instructions, no further conversation, and, to be honest, I did not really think about that moment for much longer. I continued living my life, and the year 2018 came to an end.

Have you ever had a similar experience where God gave you a word, but there was no real follow-up? I have heard the Lord speak in my life before, but never this vague. When I heard Him in the past, it was noticeably clear and concise. However, this time was different, and it reminded me of the story of Abraham.

We are first introduced to Abraham in Genesis 11, and at that time, he was called Abram. Terah (Abram's father), Abram, Sarai (his wife), and Lot (his nephew) were headed to the land of Canaan but settled in Haran. It was in Haran that Abram's father died. Genesis 12:1-4 says, "The Lord had said to Abram, "Leave your native country, your relatives, and your father's family, and go to the land that I will show you. I will make you into a great nation. I will bless you and make you famous, and you will be a blessing to others. I will bless those who bless you and curse those who treat you with contempt. All the families on earth will be blessed through you." So Abram departed as the Lord had instructed, and Lot went with him. Abram was seventy-five years old when he left Haran."

Many people have heard this Scripture before, and it is often talked about in church. If this is your first time hearing it, I encourage you to read it on your own as we discuss it in this book. Abraham is a great example of displaying faith and being obedient to God. Obedience always first requires faith. I am not sure about you, but I do not know if I would have been able to leave everything I have ever known: my family, home, comfort, and then set out to an unknown destination. This story had so inspired me because Abraham just got up and left. To our knowledge, it does not say he asked any questions. It just said that he "departed." One of my prayers was to always have faith like Abraham. However, as I have heard people say many times, "Be careful what you pray for."

On Sunday, January 27th, 2019, I experienced what I now call an "Abraham moment." I define these moments as God calling you out of your own comfort zone and leading you to a place totally unknown to you. I was at home: fasting, reading a book, and minding my own business when the Holy Spirit started speaking to me. When the Holy Spirit interrupts your time and starts to speak, it is serious. I wish I could tell you I was like Samuel and answered, "Speak Lord, your servant is listening," but that would be a total lie. In fact, I did quite the opposite and tried to ignore Him. After thirty minutes, I realized I was still on the same page of my book. I recognized my plan was not working; I needed to start listening. I opened my journal, started listening, and began writing. What happened next was the beginning of my year of obedience.

I heard the words, "Erin, I want you to host a youth conference and not just any youth conference, but a city-wide conference." The Holy Spirit continued speaking and told me the title of the conference, the vision, and the topics to be covered. Now, for some people, you are probably thinking, "Erin, really, a youth conference. That's nothing!" To be honest, the more I wrote everything down, the more inadequate I felt.

I was living in Baltimore and had been involved in youth ministry at my church for the last four years, but who was I to host a youth conference? Especially in a city I did not grow up in and where I had minimal connections. I kept thinking, "God, you want me to do what now? What are people going to think? You must have me confused with someone else!" However, the only person who was confused was me. I had to go back and remind myself of these words, "Erin, 2019 will be your year of obedience." This was my chance. Would I be obedient like I told God I would?

As I continued to write down everything, I closed my journal and said to myself, "Well, I guess I am hosting a youth conference." I had no idea how I was going to plan a youth conference or fund it. I did not even know if anyone would show up. Nevertheless, I firmly believed that if God was calling me to be obedient, it was my job to say yes. He would help take care of the rest. I love the way Samuel said it in 1 Samuel 15:22: "What is more pleasing to the Lord: your burnt offerings and sacrifices or your obedience to his voice? Listen! Obedience is better than sacrifice, and submission is better than offering the fat of rams."

My questions to you are: "Which area of your life is God calling you to be obedient? Will you answer the call?" For me, it was hosting a youth conference. For you, it may be writing a book, starting a ministry, applying for school, writing a business plan, forgiving someone who hurt you. Everyone's obedience looks different, but we are all called to be obedient. Will you answer the call today? If your answer is, "Yes, I will be obedient to what God has called me to do," then know that I am excited for you. I will also be praying for you as you take the next step, and I hope this book will give you some guidance from my own experiences as you walk in obedience.

If you are uncertain of what God may be calling you to do, He will reveal it to you in His perfect timing. I pray you will continue to seek His kingdom first. If your answer is "no" due to fear, inadequacy, or for whatever reason you may have, also know that I will be praying for you. I also want to leave you with this question: "Who is missing out due to your lack of obedience?"

Chapter 2
This is Bigger than You

When you decide to be obedient to what God is calling you to do, you must remember that this is bigger than you. In Genesis 12:3, God told Abraham, "All the families on earth will be blessed through you." This Scripture shows that Abraham's obedience was not about him, but it was about the people who would be blessed through him. When God is calling us into obedience, we may feel like we need to have everything together before we start. We need the right degree, the right connections, financial stability, and other things; if we do not, we do an excellent job of talking ourselves out of it.

In my case, I felt inadequate. Yes, I had served in youth ministry for a while, but I had no experience planning events. I also did not have connections to any youth other than those I served on Sunday. One Friday night, God showed me I could not allow my feelings of inadequacy to stop me from what He was calling me to do.

In December 2018, I began hosting "Youth Girls Nights" at my house. I wanted to continue to engage with the youth outside of the church in a safe environment. As I look back now, it is interesting to see how God was already preparing me for something that would come later. During a Friday night in February, as we were sitting around talking, the girls were sharing some of the struggles their friends were facing. While they were sharing, I heard the Holy Spirit whisper, "These are the girls I need you to reach." It was at that moment I realized that what God was calling me to do had nothing to do with me. Everything was about the youth God would allow me to minister to and the lives He would change. Fast forward to a year later; I now understand that concept more than ever.

There are people waiting on you to be obedient to what God has called you to do. It will not be an easy process, and, at times, the reminder of why you are doing it will be the only thing that keeps you going. For me, it was remembering that there is a next generation God wanted me to reach. This reminder helped, especially on the days when I wanted to give up, but we will get into that in a later chapter.

I wonder if Abraham fully understood what God meant when He said, "All families on this earth will be blessed because of you." Abraham's obedience to leave his relatives and home was, again, so much bigger than him; literally, because of his obedience, we (yes, yourself included) are all blessed. One man's obedience led to all families on earth being blessed.

What if I told you that your step into obedience could have an impact on the world? You may be thinking, "I doubt that," but it is a matter of perspective. By choosing to walk in obedience, you could be blessing one person, and that person may then go and bless five persons, and then those five persons may bless another twenty-five persons and so on. However, it could all have started with your choice to answer the call. I know this may sound scary, and a lot of people say "no" because of fear. They do not want to handle this type of pressure and are afraid of doing it all alone. To be honest, you are exactly right; you cannot accomplish something so big in your own power. Nonetheless, I have good news for you, "You are not alone because God is with you, and I can prove it."

God said to Abraham, "Go to a land that I will show you." Can you see it yet? Sure, I did not see it at first either. At first glance at this passage, I thought that when God called Abraham to leave his country and family, he would be doing this alone. If you look deeper, you will see Abraham was not alone at all. When I began to really dive into the text, God revealed to me that if He was going to "show" Abraham the land, it means He had to "be with" Abraham. Abraham was not walking in obedience alone.

When God is calling you to do something that is bigger than you, He is not calling you to do it alone. He will be with you, just as He was with Abraham. Not only is He with you, but He will also show you the way. You do not always need to know the next step, have the next answer, or have everything

21

all together. Just as God was with Abraham, He will be with you and will be guiding you. Yes, this thing God has called you to do may be bigger than you, but it is not bigger than our God. You must trust that He will show you the way.

Chapter 3
Confirmation

You have started on your journey into what God has called you to do. The book has been started, the loan documents have been submitted, the business plan has been written, but suddenly, doubt starts to creep in. If you are like me, it may sound like this: "I am in way over my head" or "What made me think I could do this?" Does any of this sound familiar? I wonder if Abraham felt the same way. If we continue in Genesis 12, we see that Abraham departed as the Lord instructed. He took his wife and nephew along with their wealth and headed for the land of Canaan. Once Abraham arrived in Canaan, something interesting happened, which reminds me that God is always with us.

Genesis 12:7 states: "Then the Lord appeared to Abram and said, I will give this land to your descendants. And Abram built an altar there and dedicated it to the Lord, who had appeared to him." Earlier, we see God telling Abraham to go to a land that He would show him. Now we see that after Abraham departed and started on his journey, God confirmed

His promise. God gave Abraham confirmation! I cannot speak for Abraham, but I wonder if he was starting to get a little anxious once he left his comfort zone. If I was Abraham, I think it would have sounded like this: "God, did I hear You correctly? Did You really tell me to leave, or did I hear You wrong?" Since God created us, God knows exactly how we think and knows we need confirmation to continue our journey.

I received my own confirmation about a week and a half after God had given me the vision for the conference. Since that time, I only told one person about the conference because I was honestly afraid to speak the words that God gave me out loud. Even though I told God I was going to be obedient, I was not ready for the world to know. I first needed confirmation. So, I arranged a meeting with wise counsel, who also happened to be my pastor. I told him the vision God had given me, and he confirmed many things God had said. I departed the meeting more scared than when I arrived because now it was officially out there. The words were spoken out of my mouth, and I knew I could no longer sit around. I needed to put my plans into action now that I had received confirmation.

My question to you is, "What did your confirmation look like?" Confirmation can look differently for everyone; it can appear in numerous ways. Confirmation can come through wise counsel, such as in my case, but it may also come through Scripture, prayer, visions, worship, etc. The important thing to remember is that you need to have confirmation.

My confirmation came not only through wise counsel, but the week before January 27th, I literally came across the Scripture verses Deuteronomy 31:6,8 three times. Deuteronomy 31:6 reads: "So be strong and courageous! Do not be afraid and do not panic before them. For the Lord your God will personally go ahead of you. He will neither fail you nor abandon you." During that time, I remember journaling and specifically asking the Lord what He was trying to confirm to me. I remember the Lord saying, "Erin, where I am calling you, I need you to hold on to this Scripture. I will neither fail you nor abandon you." Little did I know that three days later, He would give me the vision.

Let us return to Genesis 12:7 for a quick moment because I do not want you to miss something when it comes to confirmation. The second part of Genesis 12:7 states: "And Abram built an altar there and dedicated it to the Lord, who had appeared to him." Building an altar was a very common tradition in the Old Testament and was the most common image of worship. The first time "altar" was mentioned in the Bible was in the story of Noah, which is found earlier in Genesis. In Genesis 8:20, after the flood was over, and once Noah left the boat, he built an altar to the Lord. Abraham did the same thing after the Lord had appeared to him. So, my question to you is: "When you get these confirmations, are you building your altars?"

Altars were normally made from items such as stone, brick, or wood, and they were places for memorials and sacrifices. I am not asking you to build an altar as they did in the Old Testament, but it is an option. What I am asking is: How are you remembering and giving God the praise once you received your confirmation? I am able to write this book because, during my year of obedience, multiple friends told me to ensure I was journaling as a reminder of all the things God was doing in my life. While we are on this journey, we cannot forget about the One who saw us fit in the first place and has been walking beside and continues to walk beside us. When the tests come, we can look back at the altars and remember the confirmations.

Chapter 4
When the Tests Come

I hate taking tests! For as long as I can remember, I have not been a good test-taker. Unfortunately, tests are not something we can avoid in life, and they always seem to pop up. Abraham was faced with a test soon after his journey started, which would have been the last thing I expected. It is like saying to God, "I am doing everything You told me to do, so why am I experiencing a test?" You think everything should go smoothly, right? Well, unfortunately, that is wrong thinking. We are never exempted from going through tests, and that included Abraham.

Genesis 12:10 states, "At that time a severe famine struck the land of Canaan, forcing Abram to go down to Egypt, where he lived as a foreigner." The word famine has two definitions. The first definition is, "extreme scarcity of food," and the second definition is "a shortage." In Abraham's case, we are dealing with famine as an extreme scarcity of food. However, for most of us, we may see it as having a shortage. You may have a shortage of funds, resources, or support. The area I want to bring to your attention is that this famine tested Abraham's faith and obedience.

When Abraham traveled to Egypt, he was faced with what I believe was a dilemma. Abraham's wife, Sarah, was exceptionally beautiful, and he thought if the Egyptians knew she was his wife, they would kill him. So, Abraham devised a plan to tell the Egyptians that Sarai was his sister in order to spare his life. Although Abraham's life was spared, Pharaoh did something I do not think Abraham could have predicted. Pharaoh took Sarah as his wife. While listening to this dilemma, there are two things that really stuck out to me. First, Abraham never consulted God before coming up with his story. Secondly, Abraham was acting out of fear. When you put these two things together, the outcome is never a good one. In previous chapters, God told Abraham He would give the land to his descendants (offspring), but how would that promise come forth if Sarah was no longer his wife? When Abraham operated out of fear and did not consult God, he was putting his promise from God in jeopardy. This is something I know all too well!

At the beginning of March, I went home for a family visit and began to share the vision for the youth conference with them. This was my first time sharing it with all my family, and most of them were very encouraging, while others were not as optimistic. I remember being bombarded with questions like: "How are you going to pay for this? What noteworthy speakers will be in attendance? Will people actually come, and what will happen if they don't?" Looking back, I know all the concerns were out of love, but I did not see it that way at the time. The issues in my mind I was already battling with were now being brought to the forefront and, like Abraham, fear and anxiety began to creep in.

I remember sitting in the back of the car after having this discussion and wanting to cry. I then began to second guess everything I had done within the last month. Did I hear from God correctly? Maybe I heard Him wrong and was moving too fast. I allowed my fear to get the best of me, and I did not even consult with God to ask Him what He thought. That evening I was one hundred percent ready to cancel the conference, but then I remembered that I made a deposit on the venue the day before. Thank God for that deposit! If it was not for the down payment, this book would not be written because my obedience would have ended there. Just like in Abraham's story, God came through and protected His promise.

Genesis 12:17-19 states, "But the Lord sent terrible plagues upon Pharaoh and his household because of Sarai, Abram's wife. So Pharaoh summoned Abram and accused him sharply. "What have you done to me?" he demanded. "Why didn't you tell me she was your wife? Why did you say, 'She is my sister,' and allow me to take her as my wife? Now then, here is your wife. Take her and get out of here!"

This story is so powerful and shows God's grace toward Abraham. Even though Abraham did not consult with the Lord and took matters into his own hands due to fear, God still came through to fulfill His promise. It is encouraging to know that God will continue to intercede on our behalf despite our own human failures.

In my own story, I believe putting the deposit down on the venue was God interceding on my behalf. God knew the test I would face, and he was not going to allow me to fail. My question to you is: "How will you handle the pressure when the tests come?" Did you notice I said "when" and not "if"? I can promise you that the tests will come; however, we serve a God who will always intercede on our behalf. So, remember, you will face tests while walking in your obedience but be encouraged; God will be there to intervene when you need Him. If you should learn something from Abraham's story as well as my own, it is the importance of always consulting with the Lord. Also, do not allow fear to consume you as you face your own tests. This will help you protect your peace.

Chapter 5
Protect Your Peace

One of the hardest but most important lessons I learned when walking in obedience is the importance of protecting your peace. When God has called you higher or into a new season, you will learn that, unfortunately, not everyone is able to go with you, and not everyone wants to see you succeed. The hard part about this reality is that these could be the people closest to you and/or the people you have known your whole life. Therefore, as you move into your calling, you may see a shift in people. This may cause you to respond, which is exactly what Abraham had to do once he left Egypt.

Genesis 13:5-7 states, "Lot, who was traveling with Abram, had also become very wealthy with flocks of sheep and goats, herds of cattle, and many tents. But the land could not support both Abram and Lot with all their flocks and herds living so close together. So disputes broke out between the herdsmen of Abram and Lot. (At that time Canaanites and Perizzites were also living in the land.)" If we had to decipher what type

31

of disputes broke out, what comes to your mind? I am thinking jealousy, comparison, competition, and fear. They both had an increase in wealth, so they started to become rivals. There are so many possibilities, but whatever the reasoning was, it caused problems.

When you begin to walk in obedience, do not be surprised if conflicts begin to develop with people and in places where you feel the most comfortable. Remember, not everyone wants to see you succeed and achieve the plans God has for you. We can take a lesson from how Abraham handled this problem. Genesis 13:8-9 reads, "Finally Abram said to Lot, "Let's not allow this conflict to come between us or our herdsmen. After all, we are close relatives! The whole countryside is open to you. Take your choice of any section of the land you want, and we will separate. If you want the land to the left, then I'll take the land on the right. If you prefer the land on the right, then I'll go to the left." What I found most interesting in this Scripture was in the beginning when Abram said, "Let's not allow this conflict to come between us or our herdsmen." I believe Abraham knew the importance of having peace, and he knew this conflict was not healthy. It was more important for him to have peace than conflict. This is a word! In your own life, are you quick to choose conflict, or are you quick to promote peace?

This is an area of my life I have not been the best at. So many times, I chose the desire to be "right" over having peace. I would participate in the conflict, which would lead to even bigger conflict. In the end, I learned that being right was not worth the peace that was lost. Abraham, on the other hand, chose the latter. Especially due to their relationship, Abraham decided he wanted to have peace more than conflict, so he had a choice to make. Despite this difficult decision, I believe he felt the best way to avoid conflict and to promote peace was to separate.

Separation, for some, may be an easy decision, but let us not forget Lot was Abraham's nephew. If we go back earlier in Genesis, I think their family relationship was probably much closer. In Genesis 11, we see Lot's father, Haran had died in Ur and Lot was living with his grandfather, Terah, and Abram and Sarai. When God called Abram to leave his native country, Lot also went with him. I would assume that Abram probably raised Lot as his own son.

I believe this is important to understand because no one is off-limits when it comes to protecting your peace. However, depending on your age, I am not giving permission for parents to separate from their children and children to separate from their parents because of disputes. Nice try though! What I am saying is, even when the closest people to us, those who we love and respect, are causing us conflict, this may be a sign to separate. Now this separation could be for a season or longer, but it is separation nonetheless. Separation can also look different for many people. In Abraham's case, he needed to physically separate himself from Lot, but my situation was different.

It was after a family conversation that I learned I needed to protect my peace. I was having a really good day; everything was falling into place with the conference, and I was excited to share all God was doing. However, I was talking to someone on the phone, and the conversation did not go the way I planned. I remember sharing the updates with the individual, and when I was finished, I was being asked a number of questions. One thing, in particular, I recall they said was, "I just don't want you to blame God if this fails." After the conversation was over, I remember feeling so deflated.

Now, this was not the first time that something unsettling like this was said, but I really wanted their approval. However, after this conversation, I learned it was more important for me to protect my peace than it was for me to seek validation. I decided I would no longer share any updates about the conference with this person from then on. This decision was not an easy one to make. The conference was so important to me, and I really wanted to be able to share my updates, but I could not allow individuals to take my peace. Looking back now, I do not believe this person did it maliciously; rather, it was the individual's way of trying to protect me. Even so, I knew I had to protect my own peace. Like Abraham, to prevent conflict, separation was the key.

The words of my mother also helped me to protect my peace. She said, "Remember, God did not give them the vision; He gave it to you!" I believe Abraham also understood this phrase. Abraham knew the promise God gave him; he knew the conversations he had with God and the vision he saw. Therefore, even though he may not have wanted to separate

34

from Lot, he knew separation was the key in promoting his peace. Not everyone will understand the importance of separation, but, at times, you must decide what is most important to you. What would have happened if Lot and Abraham stayed together, and the conflict between them escalated? Would that lack of peace impact the promise God had given Abraham? I believe it would have, and Abraham possibly knew this. As you continue to walk in obedience, do not be surprised if separation occurs. It may hurt for the moment, but the peace found because of the separation will prove to be worth it in the end.

Chapter 6
Walk, Don't Run

One of my favorite things to do, especially on a nice spring day, is to go for a walk or a bike ride. It helps to clear my mind as I look at the beauty of God's creation. As a former track athlete, I know there is a huge difference between walking and running. One takes a lot more effort than the other, and you are also prone to fatigue a whole lot quicker. When it comes to the term "obedience," we are called to "walk in obedience," not "run in obedience." However, I believe my tail took off running.

It was two months into the conference vision, and I was fully engulfed in the planning process. The conference was set for August 17th, 2019. I had all my speakers lined up, the venue was booked, our website and marketing had launched, and I also secured a decorator and worship band. I realize now that when God wants you to move, it can happen swiftly. I am the type of person who wants things to happen now and fast. This is exactly why I enjoyed being a sprinter because the race was over quickly. However, I learned the hard way that being obedient is more of a marathon and not a sprint. I was doing a lot of things for God, but I was not taking time for myself to rest. I do not believe God wants you to get burnt out, even if it is doing things for Him.

In choosing to obey, we often want things to happen fast, but God really takes His own time. God wants us to walk instead of run. When we walk, we are able to take in all of our surroundings and the intricate details. We see and are aware of His divine connections, His God-winks (as I call reminders that He sees you), His protection, and all the lessons He is teaching us through the process. However, if we decide to run, we may miss it all. During this season, I had to learn that I needed to walk and not run, which also included allowing myself to rest.

Abraham also had what I believe is the "walk and not run lesson." We pick up with Abraham's story again in Genesis 13:14-17, which says: After Lot had gone, the Lord said to Abram, "Look as far as you can see in every direction—north and south, east and west. I am giving all this land, as far as you can see, to you and your descendants as a permanent possession. And I will give you so many descendants that, like the dust of the earth, they cannot be counted! Go and walk through the land in every direction, for I am giving it to you." Did you catch what God told Abram to do? He told him to "walk." While reading and dissecting this passage, I thought it was interesting that God told Abraham to first look around. This is so powerful because even in Scripture, God was telling Abraham: "I want you to stop and see what is around you."

Do you feel like you are at a place where God may be telling you to stop and look around? God was definitely telling me to do this. I was getting so caught up in writing my next email and scheduling the next meeting that I did not take time to look up and look around. Sometimes we get so focused on what God is calling us to do that we forget to be present in the moment. We also forget to ask God what He is trying to teach us in the moment. When you are in the process of writing your business plan, applying for school, or recording the record, do not be so focused on running to the next thing. Take time to absorb everything during the moment.

God's next instruction to Abraham was so profound. First, Abraham was to look in every direction: north and south, east, and west; then God told him to walk in every direction. He did not tell him to jog, and He did not tell him to run; instead, he told him to walk. I believe God needed to tell Abraham to walk the land first because God needed to prepare him for the promise ahead. As Abraham walked the entire piece of land, he was becoming more familiar and knowledgeable about it. This is what happens when we walk and not run. If you should ever go on a long walk (which I believe most of you have), really look around and take in your surroundings, then you will start to notice various things. You may notice parts of your walk may be a little more uneven than others. It may include some hills, some turns, and flatter areas; you begin to learn about the environment. You will probably notice things you had never seen before.

Now some of you may say: "You can do the same things when you run." In response to that statement, I would say, "You don't get the same effect." When you are out running, you have an awareness of your environment, but other factors play a part. First, you have to worry about your breathing; then you notice your heart begins to beat faster; you become thirsty and start to worry about your form, and then fatigue starts to kick in. While you are running, your internal factors begin to outweigh your awareness of the external factors. When God instructed Abraham to walk through the land, He wanted him to understand and see the external factors of all He was doing. He did not want Abraham's internal factors to play a part because that could have very well cost him or slowed down the promise.

My questions to you are: "Will you walk instead of run? Will you avoid being caught up in all the things you are doing for God, that you miss out on all the things God may be trying to teach or show you in the process? Will you take time to rest?"

During my season of planning for the conference, I took a one week vacation with my mom and we headed to the beach. I remember during that vacation, God specifically told me I needed to take a day to rest. During that day, He did not want me to do anything for the conference. It is funny as I look back on it now. During that day of rest, do you know what I did? I took a walk. God really does have a way of bringing things full circle. During my vacation, I was able to take time to spend in His presence, spend time with my mom, and was able to leave that week of vacation rejuvenated. Not only that, but

God also spoke to me more about the conference when I took time to rest in Him.

Therefore, I pray that as you continue to walk in obedience, you will continue to do just that; you will walk. You will look and walk in every direction and continue to be prepared for all God is going to do by you answering the call.

Chapter 7

Get Comfortable Being Uncomfortable

I enjoy being comfortable because it is easy and familiar. Comfortable is what you are used to, and it is something to which you can relate. When we met Abraham at the beginning of Genesis, I believe he was comfortable with where his life was. He was living in his native country, surrounded by family, and experiencing wealth. If you ask me, this sounds pretty comfortable. I am not sure where you are in life, but when God spoke to me in January 2019, I was also comfortable. I had a loving family and wonderful friends, a career I loved, and a passion for youth ministry. I still had desires and prayers I had not yet seen come to pass, but I was comfortable with my life overall.

As I have grown in my faith in this last year, I firmly understand now that God does not want us to live a life that is too comfortable. When we get comfortable with life, we tend to rely more on ourselves and our own strength. However, when we are forced to be "uncomfortable," we must totally rely on God. I remember talking with one of my friends during the season of planning for my conference, and I recall her saying, "Erin, you need to get comfortable being uncomfortable." When she said that to me, it was the last thing I wanted to hear, but it was exactly what I needed to hear. So, I am telling you exactly what my friend told me: "Get comfortable being uncomfortable!"

In obeying the call God has placed on your life, you are also saying yes to living uncomfortable. As we have seen so far in Abraham's life, his journey was far from comfortable. Since the beginning, Abraham was called away from everything that was familiar to him. He was called to leave his home and family to go to an area that God would show him. This must have made Abraham extremely uncomfortable. So, when Abraham said yes to God, he chose a life that was uncomfortable. When you choose to walk in obedience, you are choosing to be uncomfortable. However, it is up to you to walk fully in it.

I returned from my vacation on April 8th, 2019, and I remember praying the night before. It was during that prayer that I was telling the Lord that I would do anything for Him. I was in the season of planning the conference, and I was willing to do anything for God. As I mentioned earlier, you need to be careful what you pray for because God hears all your prayers. God woke me up early the next morning and said to me, "Okay, then do it."

Just to backtrack a little, a few months before this happened, I felt the Lord telling me to apologize to someone from my childhood. He was asking me to apologize for something that happened over twenty years ago, but I kept making excuses like, "That was so long ago" or "What would I look like apologizing now?" God even allowed our paths to cross, but I would not make the first step because it made me uncomfortable. Now, please do not judge me. I am walking out my faith just like you, and I do not always get it right. However, I am thankful we serve a God of second chances.

Returning to the story, God woke me up that day and said, "Okay, then do it!"

I was thinking, *"God, I know you don't mean what I think you mean."*

He then said to me, "Erin, you said you'll do anything, but you still haven't done what I have been asking you to do."

In that instant, God got my whole life together. There was a choice that needed to be made. Would I continue to be comfortable, or would I take a step forward in being uncomfortable? I decided to step out of my comfort zone, and I reached out to the individual and apologized. That was probably one of the most uncomfortable things I had ever done. However, I learned that when God has chosen you for an assignment, you must choose to live a life that is uncomfortable.

Since that time, I started to pray: "God, if it is needed to do Your will and to expand Your kingdom, then Lord make me uncomfortable." I was so afraid to make this declaration as I knew I would be placed in circumstances that made me uncomfortable. This is exactly what happened. I have encountered so many instances where I was made uncomfortable, whether it was meeting with new individuals, being engaged with other people in leadership, or talking about sex and relationships with youth on Sunday mornings. However, as I continue to study Abraham's story, I realize that he lived a life that was uncomfortable. Now the interesting thing about comfort levels is that everyone's level is different. For Abraham, it was being called away from his home and family. For me, it was about reconciliation, amongst other things. Yours will look more different than mine. However, what I know for sure is, once you decide to walk in obedience, you must get comfortable being uncomfortable.

Since saying yes to God on January 27th, 2019, I live an uncomfortable life, not just in ministry. I see it in all aspects of my life, from my career to my relationships and even in business. Even writing this book was uncomfortable. However, as I mentioned at the beginning of this chapter, when you are doing things that make you uncomfortable, you can no longer rely on your own strength; you must rely fully on God.

To be honest, I still dislike being put in positions that make me uncomfortable, but if I decided to always be comfortable, where would that lead me? Being uncomfortable not only helps you to grow, but it also allows you to fully trust God. Even when I am uncomfortable, I know God is with me, and it is not about me anyway.

Chapter 8
What About Me, God?

I was in the middle of planning the conference, and I continued walking in obedience to God by listening to Him, walking with Him, and serving Him. Nevertheless, I was starting to feel as though He had forgotten about me. Maybe you are currently going through a season similar to this. You have decided to answer the call, and you are walking in obedience and doing all the things God has called you to do. However, there are desires and prayers you have yet to see fulfilled. If you are feeling like this, do not be discouraged because you are not alone. I have experienced the exact feeling, which had me thinking, "Okay, God, I am doing all that You are asking me to do, but what about me? What about the things I desire and hope for?" All I can tell you is, "You are not alone. God hears you!"

I feel encouraged when I know I am not the only one going through things, especially when those things are pertaining to doing God's will. Therefore, when we continue Abraham's story in Genesis, we see him having a very real conversation with God. He was asking God the same question we tend to ask Him: "What about me?" Genesis 15:1-3 states: Some time later, the Lord spoke to Abram in a vision and said to him, "Do not be afraid, Abram, for I will protect you, and your reward will be great." But Abram replied, "O Sovereign Lord, what good are all your blessings when I don't even have a son? Since you've given me no children, Eliezer of Damascus, a servant in my household, will inherit all my wealth. You have given me no descendants of my own, so one of my servants will be my heir." As I previously mentioned, it is reassuring to know that someone is going through the same thing as you. I found it even more encouraging to know that Abraham, who was solely picked by God, experienced some of the same feelings I was now experiencing.

Abraham had been obedient to God from the beginning, but at this particular moment, we really see where his humanity came through. We see that Abraham desired a son. He heard God repeat the promise He had given him in the beginning, but Abraham responded, "What good are your blessings when I don't even have a son?" So, basically, Abraham was saying that yes, he heard the promises, and they are great, but he was promised descendants, yet he had no child. Have you ever asked God a similar question? God, your blessings are great, but when will I get married? When will I have a child? When will I get the promotion? When will I buy that house? When will my promise be fulfilled?

If you are feeling that way right now, know that it is okay. God can handle your questions and your frustration the same way He handled Abraham's. God responded to Abraham in Genesis 15:4-6 by stating: "No, your servant will not be your heir, for you will have a son of your own who will be your heir." Then the Lord took Abram outside and said to him, "Look up into the sky and count the stars if you can. That's how many descendants you will have!" And Abram believed the Lord, and the Lord counted him as righteous because of his faith." God reminded Abraham that His promise will be fulfilled, and Abram believed the Lord.

Will you believe God, just as Abraham did? Will you believe that God's promise for you will come to pass? It is interesting that even though God told Abraham the promise would be fulfilled, he left out one essential fact, and that was "when." He did not tell him exactly when it would happen. Also, I do not mean to spoil the ending of the story for you, but Abraham received the son he was promised. His name was Isaac. Do you know how long it was until this promise was fulfilled? It was twenty-five years. Yes, twenty-five years after God initially gave Abram the promise, Isaac was born. Twenty-five years is a long time to me. Nevertheless, we serve the Author of time, so twenty-five years to God is nothing.

2 Peter 3:8 states, "But you must not forget this one thing, dear friends: A day is like a thousand years to the Lord, and a thousand years is like a day." So my question to you, which is a question I had to ask myself, is: "Will you continue to be obedient to what God has called you to do, even if you are yet to see the promise?" I think we often get so caught up in ourselves and what we want God to do for us that we forget it

51

is not about us in the first place. We are just the vessels He chose to use.

I remember so clearly that whenever I was "in my feelings," God would remind me, "It's not always about you." In my case, it was about the girls He wanted me to reach through the conference. When we begin to put things into perspective and look at the big vision God gave us, the same way God showed it to Abraham, and he believed, we also can choose to believe the Lord.

I want to remind you that God has not forgotten you or the desires of your heart. God keeps His promises, and He will fulfill everything He said. I love Psalm 126:5, which says, "Those who plant in tears will harvest with shouts of joy." So, be encouraged today and know that all you are doing is not in vain; the planning, studying, writing, and saving are not useless. Everything you are planting with tears will come back in a harvest that is exceedingly, abundantly, above all you can ask or imagine.

Remember, it took Abraham twenty-five years, but he finally received his promise. Still, during those twenty-five years, Abraham was going through the process so he would be ready to fulfill that promise. So, when you are in the process, and you are thinking, "What about me, God?" Change your perspective and instead ask, "God, what are you trying to teach me in this season?" The last thing you want to do is get the promise you have been hoping for and not be ready or able to receive it.

I pray that as you continue to walk in obedience to God, you will also allow Him to do a work in you, just as He did in Abraham. When the promise finally arrived, Abraham received it fully and he did not give up during the process.

Chapter 9
Don't Give Up

Whenever I hear the phrase "don't give up," it is sometimes followed by an eye roll. After my eye roll, I usually say: "This is hard!" I believe when you have answered the call and decide to walk into what God has called you to do, you will want to give up. If you do not experience this, well kudos to you! However, that was not my testimony. I remember very early in February, after sharing my vision with my mother, I specifically told her, "Mom, I know there will be a time while preparing for this conference that I will want to give up, but don't let me." So, I am going to tell you the exact same thing: "Don't give up!"

It was now July 2019, and I had written in my journal, "Lord, this assignment is HARD!" The conference was now a month away, and I was right in the thick of planning and trying to finalize everything. I needed God to show up. It was during this month I had literally received three rejections in one week, and I was feeling super depleted. Not only that, as the conference was approaching fast, God had me dealing with issues that were arising within me, which developed at a younger age.

It is so interesting how God works. God was calling my team and me to minister to girls; however, before we could accomplish that, we had to go back and reconcile with the younger girl who still lived in us. Honestly, it was all becoming a little overwhelming, and giving up would have been so much easier. Therefore, I had to remember what I told my mom: "I could not give up." Let me put this into terms in relation to Abraham's story: I did not want to receive Ishmael because I had given up on Isaac.

According to where we left off in Abraham's story, God had made a covenant or promise with Abraham that he would have a son, and many descendants would come through him. God gave Abraham the promise but did not tell him when the promise would come to pass. As most of us can probably relate, Abraham and his wife took matters into their own hands. They stopped believing the promise God had given them because He was taking too long. Genesis 16:1-4 states, "Now Sarai, Abram's wife, had not been able to bear children for him. But she had an Egyptian servant named Hagar. So Sarai said to Abram, "The Lord has prevented me from having children. Go and sleep with my servant. Perhaps I can have children through her." And Abram agreed with Sarai's proposal. So Sarai, Abram's wife, took Hagar the Egyptian servant and gave her to Abram as a wife. (This happened ten years after Abram had settled in the land of Canaan.) So Abram had sexual relations with Hagar, and she became pregnant. But when Hagar knew she was pregnant, she began to treat her mistress, Sarai, with contempt."

We cannot dissect this entire story because a lot is going on here, but I encourage you to read it on your own. Nevertheless, let me give you a quick summary. Sarah (Abraham's wife) told Abraham that God had prevented her from having children. She then decided to give him her servant, Hagar, as a wife so he could have a child through her. Abraham agreed, and Hagar became pregnant with Ishmael. You are probably thinking: "What in the world was Sarah thinking?" This is a crazy situation, but sometimes when we are tired of waiting, we can make poor decisions.

Abraham was given a promise from God that he would have a son. However, ten years had passed, and his wife was not able to bear children. Now, if Abraham and Sarah were like me and you, I am sure they would have conversations at the dinner table, which sounded like this: "Are you sure you heard God correctly? Did God change His mind about us? Did we do something wrong? Maybe God is mad at us." Since God was taking so long, they devised their own plan.

How do you respond when God is taking too long? Do you go and make other plans? When we do things that are not in the will of God, it leads to conflict(s), which could have been avoided. Due to Abraham's and Sarah's lack of patience, they ended up with Ishmael when it was God's plan for them to receive Isaac. Isaac is God's promise, but Ishmael was born out of their impatience. "Ishmaels" come when we give up on God's promise and decide we need to take matters into our own hands. Ishmaels also come when we decide that God is taking too long to show up, and we decide we need to speed up the process. However, if you can recall from the last chapter, God's promise to Abraham eventually came much later.

In Genesis 17:18-20, God reassured Abraham that he would have a son through his wife Sarah, but because of his old age, Abraham said: "May Ishmael live under your special blessing!" But God replied, "No—Sarah, your wife, will give birth to a son for you. You will name him Isaac, and I will confirm my covenant with him and his descendants as an everlasting covenant. As for Ishmael, I will bless him also, just as you have asked. I will make him extremely fruitful and multiply his descendants. He will become the father of twelve princes, and I will make him a great nation."

Isn't it amazing we serve a God who will still allow our promise to come, even when we try to make it happen ourselves? It is even better that God would still bless our indiscretions. Even though Abraham ended up with Ishmael, it did not discredit him from receiving Isaac. As I think about Abraham's story, I wonder if he ever thought back and said to God, "I wish I had waited on Your timing." I know there have been situations in my life where I moved ahead of God and wished I had waited on Him. If I had listened the first time, it would have saved a lot of heartaches.

I want to encourage you today that no matter where you are in your walk, do not give up on the promise or vision God has given you. I know there are days when it is hard, and you want to give up, and you wonder if God even sees you. I can promise you, He does! Here is a peek into the rest of my journal entry from that day: "Lord, this assignment is HARD. You have put so many people around me, and You said You would never leave me nor forsake me. So, I will continue to trust You, Lord, but I NEED to see You. I'm desperate for You."

My prayer for you is to remember that God will never leave you or forsake you even on the days when you want to give up. Put your trust in Him; cry out so He can know how desperately you need Him. The funny thing is, God already knows, but I think He likes to hear it. Ensure you are also surrounded by a community of believers who will not allow you to give up even when you want to. For those who may have already given up on God or moved outside of His timing, which we all have done in one season or another, please know that it is not too late for you. Your Isaac is still on his way. If God did it for Abraham, He can do the same for you.

Chapter 10
Promise Fulfilled

A braham answered the call, received confirmation, endured some tests, and took matters into his own hands. Then, after twenty-five years, he finally received the promise God had made to him at the very beginning. He received his promised son, Isaac. Isaac's name means "He laughs," and Isaac received that name because both Sarah and Abraham laughed to themselves when God revealed that they would have a baby in their old age. Have you ever researched the meaning of your name? If you have not, I suggest you should. I will tell you what my name means later in the chapter, but I believe your name also has meaning. It is also very interesting that before Abraham received his promise, both he and his wife had a name change.

In Genesis 17:4-6, after Ishmael was born, the Lord appeared to Abraham and said: "This is my covenant with you: I will make you the father of a multitude of nations! What's more, I am changing your name. It will no longer be Abram. Instead, you will be called Abraham, for you will be the father of many

61

nations. I will make you extremely fruitful. Your descendants will become many nations, and kings will be among them!" The name Abram means "exalted father" and his new name means "father of many nations." Abraham's wife, Sarai, also had her name changed to Sarah. By looking at this example, I believe when God calls you to walk in obedience, He must change something in you before you are able to receive the promise.

The name Erin means "Peace." I have also seen it as "Peaceful Ruler." For people who know me well, I am a very easy-going person. I have never been one to be involved in conflict or drama, so the definition of my name suits me well. During this season of preparing for the conference, my name did not change, but the person who I was on August 17th, 2019, was not the same person who received the vision in January. During those seven months, I do not think I have ever grown so much as a person and in my faith than in all my twenty-nine years of living. I remember posting a picture on social media following the conference and wrote: "Do you ever look at pics of yourself and not even recognize who you are?" I think God needed Abraham to have a remarkably similar experience. He needed him to be reminded of who he was; the person he was when God first called him was not the same person who was about to walk into that promise. His name would forever be changed. He was no longer who people used to call him but was now called by his promise. God told Abraham he would be a father to many nations, and his name change meant just that.

Finally, in Genesis 21:1-3, we see where God's promise came to pass, "The Lord kept his word and did for Sarah exactly what he had promised. She became pregnant, and she gave birth to a son for Abraham in his old age. This happened at just the time God had said it would. And Abraham named their son Isaac." My favorite part about this passage is: *"The Lord kept his word and did for Sarah exactly what he had promised."* This is such a wonderful reminder that we serve a God who keeps His Word.

I experienced God's promises, especially during the last week of the conference. That week was very overwhelming. I remember exactly four days before the conference, I finally broke down because I was feeling the weight and pressure of it all. Yet, during that same day, I continued to see God move.

I had to go to the venue for some details and, while at the venue, I asked if I could use what they considered their bridal suite. I needed a green room for my speakers, and the venue manager agreed to it with no increase in cost. An hour later, I went to Bible study that evening, and one of the ladies in my Bible study asked if she could supply the refreshments for our green room. How did she know I had a green room? I literally almost stopped in my tracks. An hour earlier, I did not have a green room. God did not only provide a space but also the refreshments; I was in awe. God really sees everything. This was just the beginning of His promise coming to pass.

If I could put the day of August 17th, 2019 into words, it would be exactly what was written in Genesis 21:1, with a little tweak. It would read: *"The Lord kept His Word and did for Erin exactly what He had promised.*" God showed up and showed out at that conference. He blew my mind again. That day felt totally like a dream to me as I felt like I was holding my breath all day long. I remember standing there during worship and looking at my friend and saying to her: "They came! People actually came!" From the girls in attendance to the worship band, speakers, girl talk panel, and giveaways, that day was one I will never forget. What touched me the most was not the event itself, which was absolutely amazing, but it was seeing how God came through. God did what He said He would do. We hear that phrase so often but to be able to witness it firsthand changed my life.

As I mentioned earlier in chapter one, when God first gave me this vision, I felt so inadequate to fulfill the calling God had placed on my life. God chose me to host a youth conference that would minister to young girls in a city where I did not even grow up. I had very minimal connections and little experience with event planning or public speaking. People told me I was crazy; they questioned my motives and told me not to blame God if it failed. Also, out of the twenty-one girls who attended the conference, I only knew three of them. God used me, an ordinary person who decided to say "yes" to walking in obedience to Him. By answering "yes," I, along with Abraham, experienced firsthand that God will do exactly as He promised.

Chapter 11
Greater Obedience

Eight months of preparation and the youth conference came and went. The conference was on a Saturday, and I remember going to church the next day. I remember people who had seen pictures from the conference coming up to me and saying, "It looked like a success." To be honest, those were the last words I had on my mind. I remember sitting in the back during the worship service and literally crying throughout the entire service. These were not tears of sadness but tears from the weight I was carrying on my shoulders. It is funny that while preparing for the conference, my team always talked about things pertaining to future conferences and events, and I would always, but politely, say, "Hey, who said there is going to be a next year?" However, after the conference was over, I knew how important an event like this was for the next generation.

During the conference, when I went around and talked to the different girls, many of them asked if I was going to do another conference. I had mothers who said this was so needed, and I also had individuals who were working at the venue saying how they were encouraged. Honestly, it was very overwhelming. I did not imagine saying "yes" to the vision God had given me would ever lead to this. When I woke up the next morning, the feeling I felt was not one of success, but I felt more of a burden. I felt the burden of the youth who still needed to be reached, and I could not just stop now. I felt God was calling me to greater obedience.

As I am writing, I continue to be reminded of the story of Abraham. My story, compared to Abraham's, is vastly different. However, I am reminded of his story because the lessons I learned through my experiences are very similar to lessons I believe Abraham also went through. We left off in Abraham's story with God fulfilling His promise through the child, Isaac. If I was Abraham, I would now be thinking God had finally fulfilled His promise to me, and I could now delight in the promise. However, as we conclude this part of the story, I believe God's plans were very different from what Abraham had in mind. Genesis 22:1-3 states: "Some time later, God tested Abraham's faith. "Abraham!" God called. "Yes," he replied. "Here I am." "Take your son, your only son—yes, Isaac, whom you love so much—and go to the land of Moriah. Go and sacrifice him as a burnt offering on one of the mountains, which I will show you." The next morning Abraham got up early. He saddled his donkey and took two of his servants with him, along with his son, Isaac. Then he chopped wood for a fire for a burnt offering and set out for the place God had told him about."

I have read this Scripture multiple times, and even with knowing the end of the story, it is still a difficult piece of Scripture for me to understand in multiple ways. I do not know which part of it surprises me the most. Is it that after twenty-five years, when God finally fulfilled His promise to Abraham, He would then ask him to sacrifice the same promise, or is it that Abraham was so obedient to God at that moment that he did not even question it? However, I learned here, just as I mentioned earlier, after we choose to walk in obedience, we are often called to greater obedience. As I am writing, I am seeing something in this Scripture that I had never really seen before. I believe Abraham saw it all along, and this led him to not question God but, instead, remember where he first started. Genesis 22:2 ends with: "Go and sacrifice him as a burnt offering on one of the mountains, which I will show you."

"I will show you" sounds familiar, right? This was the same phrase God said to Abraham in Genesis 12 when He told him to leave his country, family, and relatives. I wonder when Abraham heard these same words if he was reminded of God's faithfulness. This certainly would have moved him to remain obedient, even when it came to sacrificing his own son. He was able to display greater obedience because he remembered God was faithful then, and He would remain faithful.

Abraham followed God's instructions, and as he was about to sacrifice his son, an angel of the Lord stopped him and provided a ram for the sacrifice instead. Genesis 22:16-18

67

states: "This is what the Lord says: Because you have obeyed me and have not withheld even your son, your only son, I swear by my own name that I will certainly bless you. I will multiply your descendants beyond number, like the stars in the sky and the sand on the seashore. Your descendants will conquer the cities of their enemies. And through your descendants all the nations of the earth will be blessed—all because you have obeyed me."

I love this passage because it has so many things wrapped up inside of it. It all boils down to Abraham's obedience from the beginning and even greater obedience in the end. Due to Abraham's obedience, he was blessed far beyond what he had even fathomed. Even now, Abraham's story continues to encourage and remind me to walk in obedience. It is also a great reminder that when God calls you to do something, even if it requires greater obedience, He will continue to be with you; God will continue to fulfill all of His promises.

Wherever you are in your walk in obedience, I pray from both my journey as well as through the life of Abraham that you are encouraged to see that obeying God is worth it. If you are still on the fence about walking in obedience, I pray you will answer the call. If you are in the midst of walking in obedience, I pray you do not give up. If you are being called to greater obedience, I pray you are reminded of God's faithfulness throughout every season.

I mentioned earlier in the chapter that God was guiding me into greater obedience. I am currently in the process of planning our second youth conference, and I have also turned this platform into a non-profit organization. The name of the non-profit is "I Am A Child of God Inc." The mission for the non-profit originated from the same vision God gave me on January 27th, 2019: to empower our youth to be all that God has called them to be.

Each day I try my best to walk in obedience, and I honestly do not always get it right. I still question God and wonder what He is up to and why He chose me. I still have prayers and desires that I am yet to see manifest, and I have had some very serious and real conversations with God about things I continue to struggle with. However, what I have learned in my year of obedience is that God is faithful. I have seen Him come through time and time again, so I know that when you choose to obey God, He will fulfill all His promises. If God did it for Abraham, and He is doing it for me, then know that He will do it for you.

Will this be your *Year of Obedience?*

About the Author

Born in New Jersey and raised in Virginia, Erin has lived in Baltimore, Maryland for the last eight years. Erin's passion for people and her love of sports as a former college athlete led her to pursue a degree as a Doctor of Physical Therapy. Currently working as a physical therapist and center manager, Erin has always had a servant's heart and began working with youth while in high school in different capacities. Erin currently serves as the Youth Director at her church in Baltimore City. In 2019, she launched a non-profit organization called "I Am A Child of God Inc." with the mission to empower youth to be all that God has called them to be.

Erin is learning to balance career, ministry, and life. When she is not working or involved in ministry, she enjoys exercising, watching movies, and hanging out with family and friends.

Made in the USA
Middletown, DE
03 February 2021